300 FIR
FRENCH

Introduced by **OPAL DUNN**

Photographed by **GEOFF DANN**

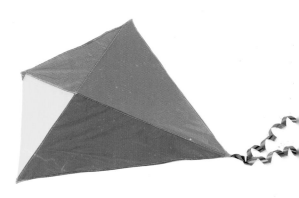

FRANCES LINCOLN

How to use this book

First words in French can be fun. Most child'
take learning a second language in their strid'
even if you yourself feel hesitant about using
speaking French, you can still begin to teach your
child. After all, you have already taught them to
speak English, so why not use some of the same
skills for French? One of the best times to start is
when your child has passed the stage of naming
things in English and is already communicating
everyday needs and feelings, but hasn't yet begun
a formal reading programme. *300 First Words in
French* takes them back to that earlier learning
stage of naming things in English – and then names
them in French.

Before you begin, explain to your child that some
people don't talk in English – they use other
languages, and one of these languages is French.
Teach them how to count in French (*un, deux,
trois*), tell them some French names of things they
will later find in the book, and how to say "yes" (*oui*)
and "no" (*non*). Say a rhyme in French, sing a song
or show them part of a television programme or
video in French.

Start the first session by naming things in French
and let your child listen, but don't expect them to
speak, to begin with. Keep the sessions short:
always stop before your child loses interest. After a
few sessions, repeat the names of familiar things a
second time, asking your child to say them aloud
with you. Begin each session with names they
already know, then introduce two or three new
ones, but never more. Finish up with a simple
game: ask them to find and show you a particular
thing in the book. Don't explain about masculine or

...e unless they ask. Let them learn the article
...e word together as one piece of language –
...rotte – *un chien* – *du pain*.

As they grow more confident, try pointing at things
...nd asking *"Qu'est-ce que c'est?"* (What's this?). If
...ey don't get the reply quite right, don't make any
comment – just repeat the correct answer, then
ask the question again. Children don't mind
repeating things – they like to have another chance
to get things right. They also have an innate ability
to refine their own pronunciation until they can get
it just like the model they hear. Don't say that
something is wrong – it might discourage them.

Later on, holding the book, say, *"Montre-moi un
crayon"* (Show me a pencil). They then have to find
the matching picture. Once they can do this, see if
they can recognise things without the book. Say,
"Va chercher un biscuit" (Go and get a biscuit), or
"Donne-moi une assiette" (Give me a plate).

Young children want to succeed and to know they
are doing well, so do include words like *bravo*
and *bien* (well done) or even *très bien* (very
well done) and praise them whenever you can.
Remember, success leads to success, and if you
can make a good start, your child will have the
confidence to go on learning French and maybe
other languages as well.

Opal Dunn

un bébé
baby

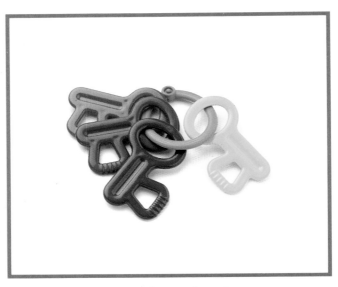

un hochet
rattle

un biberon
baby's bottle

une bavette
bib

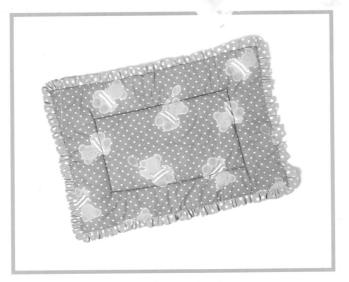

un matelas à langer
quilt

un lit d'enfant
cot

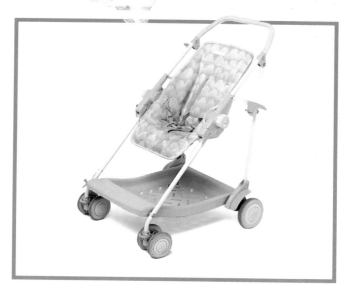

une poussette
pushchair

un landau
pram

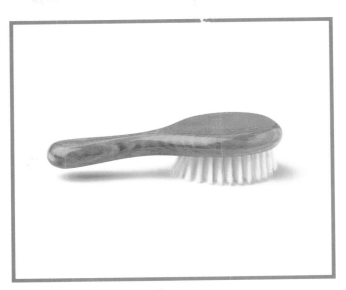

une brosse
hairbrush

un miroir
mirror

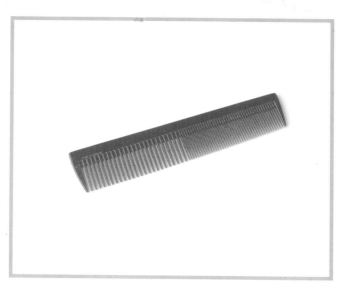

un peigne
comb

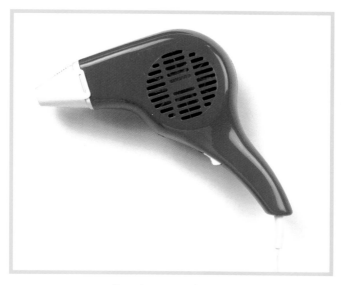

un sèche-cheveux
hairdryer

un gant
face cloth

un savon
soap

une serviette de toilette
towel

un shampoing
shampoo

une éponge
sponge

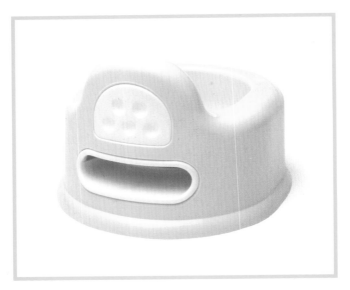

un pot
potty

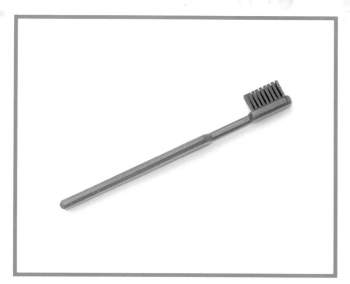

une brosse à dents
toothbrush

du dentifrice
toothpaste

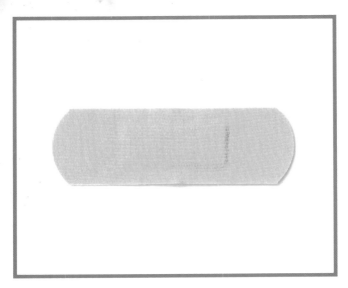

un pansement
plaster

de la ouate
cotton wool

des ciseaux à ongles
nail scissors

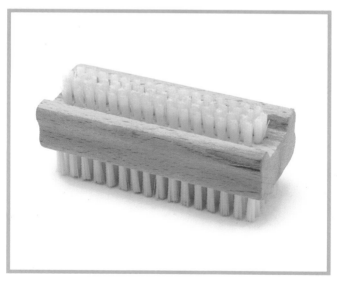

une brosse à ongles
nailbrush

une grenouillère
sleepsuit

un pyjama
pyjamas

une robe de chambre
dressing gown

un chausson
slipper

un T-shirt
vest

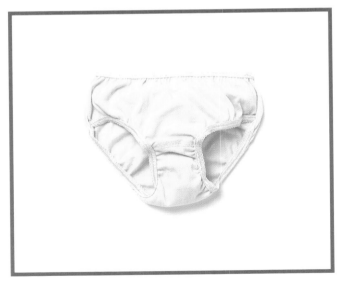

une culotte
pants

une chaussette
sock

une chaussure
shoe

une chemise
shirt

un pantalon
trousers

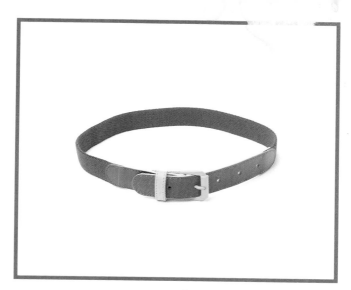

une ceinture
belt

une salopette
dungarees

un T-shirt
T-shirt

un short
shorts

un cardigan
cardigan

une robe
dress

un sweatshirt
sweatshirt

une jupe
skirt

une écharpe
scarf

un pull
jumper

un bonnet
woolly hat

un gant
glove

une moufle
mitten

un anorak
jacket

un chapeau de pluie
rainhat

un imperméable
raincoat

un parapluie
umbrella

un botillon
boot

un maillot de bain
swimsuit

une sandale
sandal

une casquette
sunhat

des lunettes de soleil
sunglasses

un seau
bucket

une pelle
spade

une raquette de ping-pong
bat

une balle
ball

un nounours
teddy bear

une poupée
doll

un pingouin
penguin

un diable
Jack-in-the-box

35

un livre d'images
picture book

un cube
alphabet block

un puzzle
jigsaw

un jeu
shape-sorter

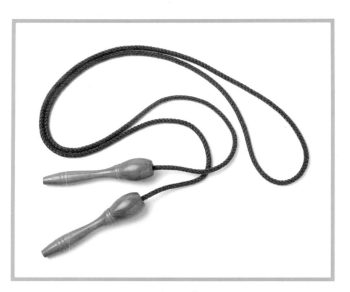

une corde à sauter
skipping-rope

un tricyle
tricycle

un ballon
balloon

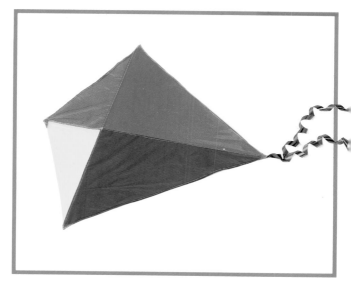

un cerf-volant
kite

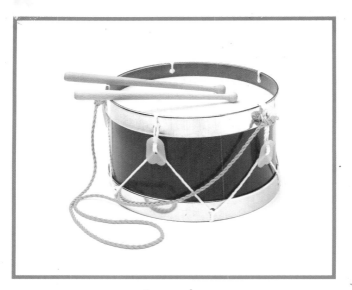

un tambour
drum

un tambourin
tambourine

une trompette
trumpet

une flûte
recorder

une guitare
guitar

un violon
violin

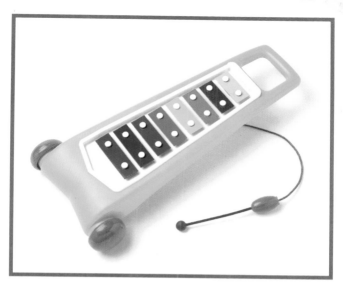

un xylophone
xylophone

un triangle
triangle

un pastel
wax crayon

un feutre
felt-tip pen

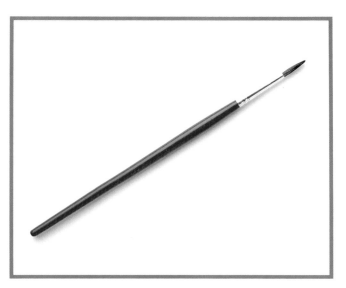

un pinceau
paintbrush

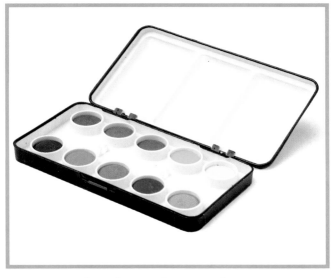

une boîte de peintures
paintbox

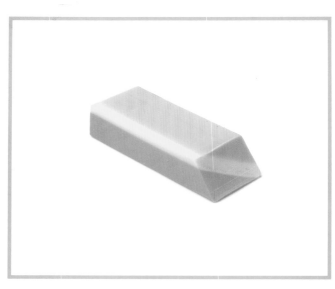

une gomme
rubber

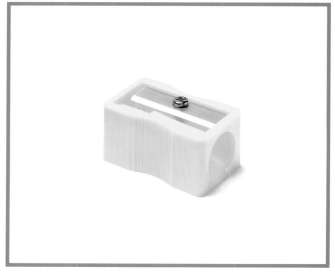

un taille-crayon
sharpener

un crayon
pencil

une trousse
pencil case

un porte-monnaie
purse

un panier
shopping basket

un sac à dos
rucksack

une valise
suitcase

des lunettes
glasses

une lampe de poche
torch

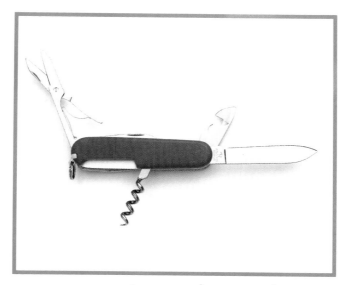

un couteau de poche
penknife

une montre
watch

un bracelet
bracelet

une bague
ring

un collier
necklace

une boucle d'oreille
earring

une pomme
apple

une orange
orange

un citron
lemon

une poire
pear

une banane
banana

des raisins
grapes

un ananas
pineapple

une pêche
peach

une mandarine
tangerine

un melon
melon

une fraise
strawberry

un abricot
apricot

une tomate
tomato

un concombre
cucumber

une laitue
lettuce

une carotte
carrot

un petit pois
pea

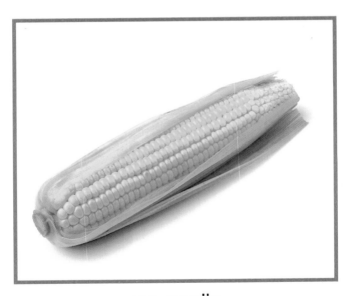

un maïs
sweetcorn

du broccoli
broccoli

un chou-fleur
cauliflower

une pomme de terre
potato

un chou
cabbage

un avocat
avocado

un oignon
onion

une glace
ice cream

une sucette
lollipop

du chocolat
chocolate

un gâteau
cake

un biscuit
biscuit

du pain
bread

un sandwich
sandwich

un petit pain
roll

du beurre
butter

du fromage
cheese

un oeuf
egg

des spaghettis
spaghetti

du miel
honey

de la confiture
jam

un jus d'orange
orange juice

du lait
milk

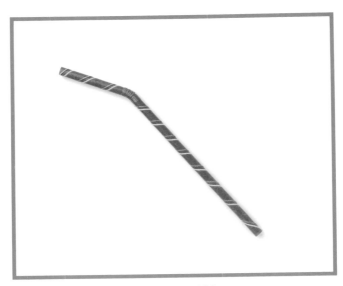

une paille
straw

un verre
glass

un gobelet
beaker

une chope
mug

une tasse

cup

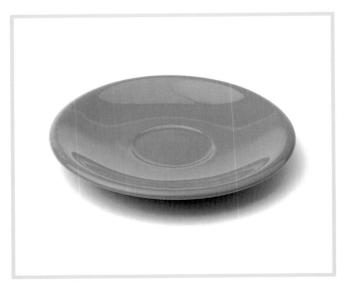

une soucoupe

saucer

une assiette creuse
bowl

une assiette
plate

un couteau
knife

une fourchette
fork

une cuillère
spoon

un coquetier
egg cup

un pot
jug

une théière
tea pot

une bouilloire
kettle

une cafetière
coffee pot

une cuillère en bois
wooden spoon

une passoire
colander

une poêle
frying pan

une casserole
saucepan

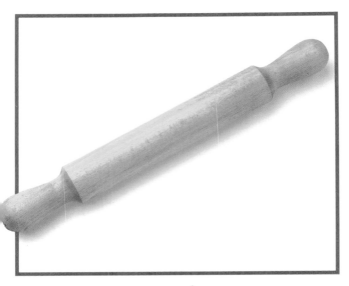

un rouleau
rolling pin

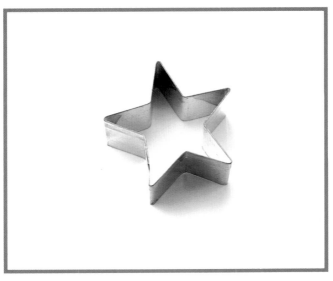

un coupe-pâte
pastry cutter

un moule
cake tin

un gant
oven glove

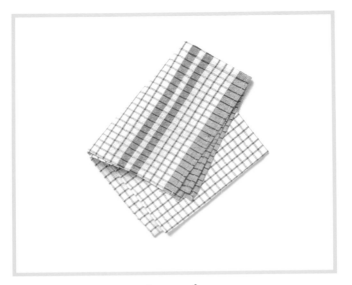

un torchon
tea towel

une bassine
washing-up bowl

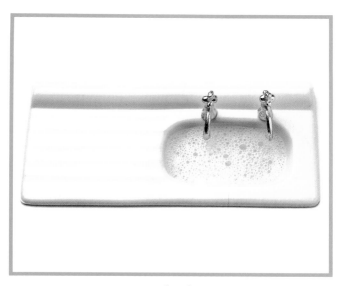

un évier
sink

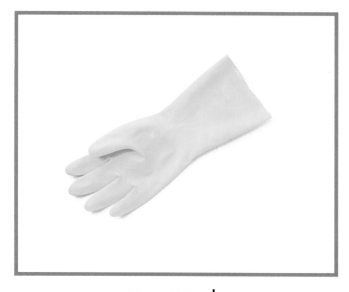

un gant
rubber glove

un moulin à poivre
pepper grinder

une salière
salt pot

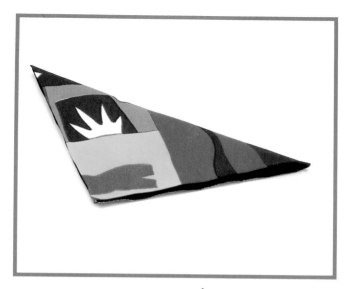

une serviette
napkin

une table
table

une chaise
chair

un bureau
desk

un fauteuil
armchair

un divan
sofa

un téléphone
telephone

une machine à calculer
calculator

un réveil
clock

un tableau
picture

une télévision
television

un ordinateur
computer

une radio
radio

un appareil-photo
camera

un oreiller
pillow

un lit
bed

un drap
sheet

une couverture
blanket

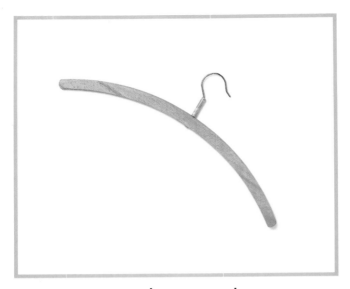

un porte-manteau
coat hanger

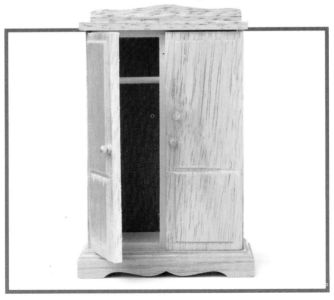

une penderie
wardrobe

un placard
cupboard

une commode
chest of drawers

une ampoule
light bulb

une lampe
lamp

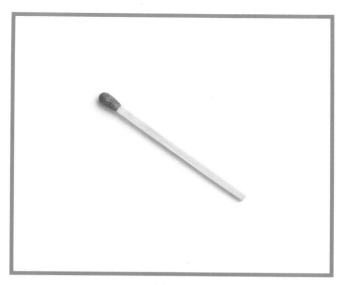

une allumette
match

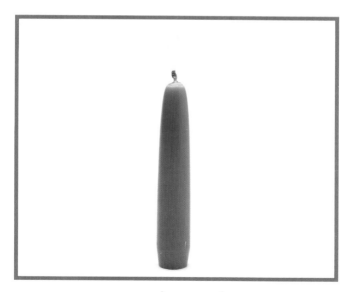

une bougie
candle

une clé
key

un trou de serrure
keyhole

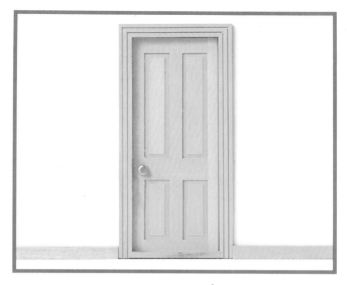

une porte
door

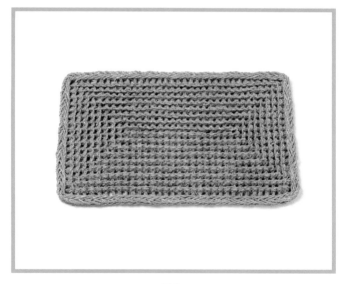

un paillasson
doormat

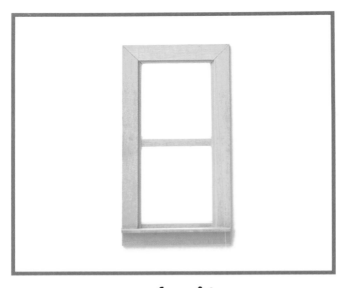

une fenêtre
window

des rideaux
curtains

un vase

vase

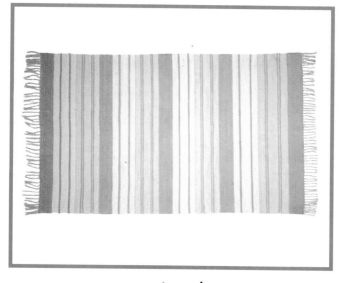

un tapis

rug

un balai
broom

un aspirateur
vacuum cleaner

une brosse
brush

une pelle
dustpan

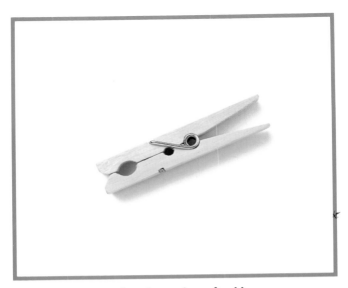

une épingle à linge
clothes peg

un panier
washing basket

un fer à repasser
iron

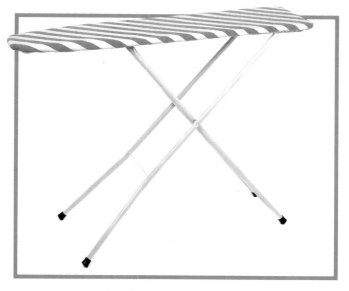

une table à repasser
ironing board

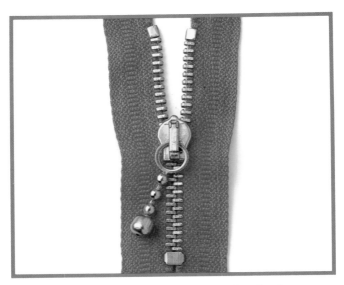

une fermeture éclair
zip

une boucle de ceinture
buckle

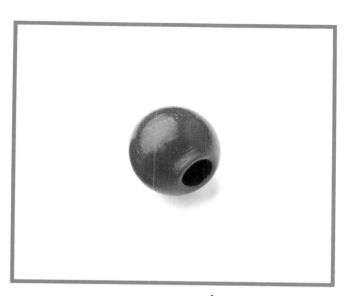

une perle
bead

un bouton
button

de la ficelle
string

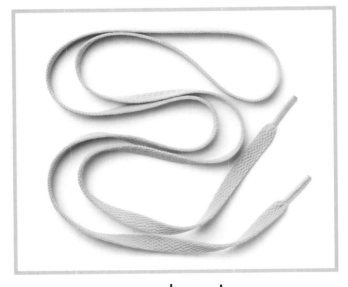

un lacet
shoelace

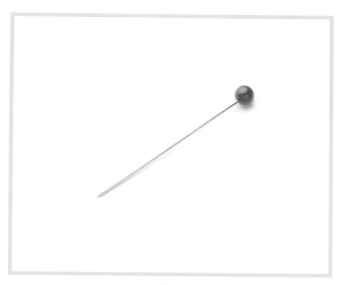

une épingle
pin

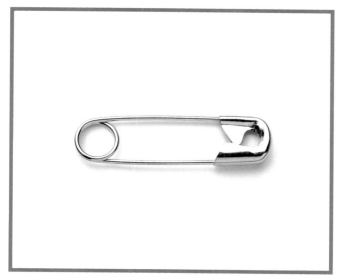

une épingle à nourrice
safety pin

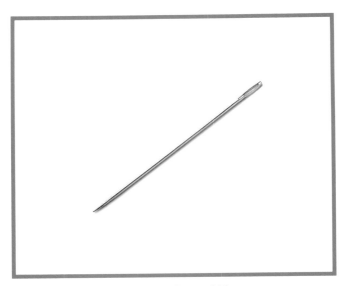

une aiguille
needle

du fil
thread

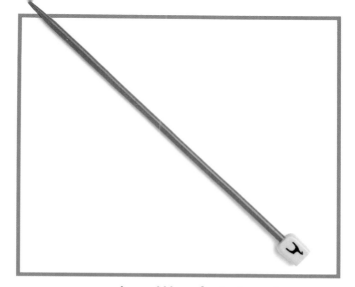

une aiguille à tricoter
knitting needle

de la laine
wool

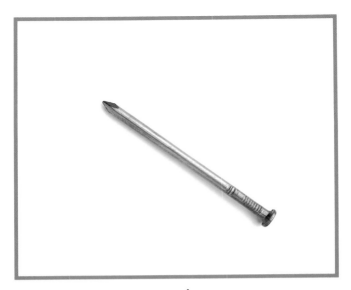

un clou
nail

un marteau
hammer

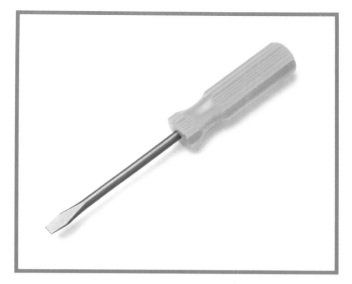

un tournevis
screwdriver

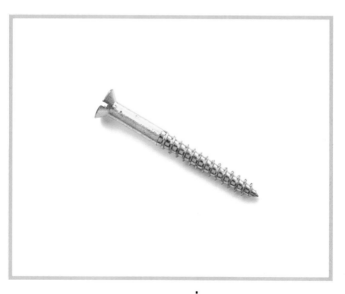

une vis
screw

un écrou
nut

une vis à écrou
spanner

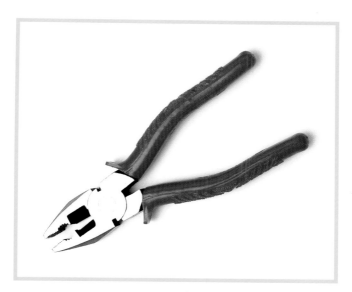

une pince
pliers

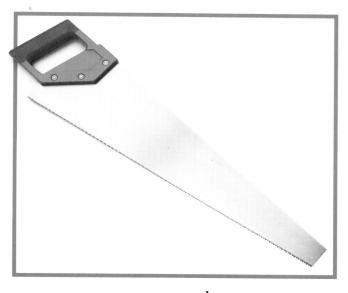

une scie
saw

une fourche
garden fork

un déplantoir
trowel

un arrosoir
watering can

un pot de fleurs
flowerpot

de l'herbe
grass

de la terre
earth

une feuille
leaf

une plante
plant

une rose

rose

une tulipe

tulip

une iris

iris

un géranium

geranium

un papillon
butterfly

une libellule
dragonfly

une fourmi
ant

une araignée
spider

un chat
cat

un chien
dog

un cheval
horse

une vache
cow

une poule
hen

un coq
cockerel

une chèvre
goat

un mouton
sheep

un âne
donkey

un cochon
pig

une oie
goose

un canard
duck

un lion
lion

un tigre
tiger

une girafe
giraffe

un panda
panda

un zèbre
zebra

un chameau
camel

un rhinocéros
rhinoceros

un éléphant
elephant

un ours
bear

un renne
reindeer

une autruche
ostrich

un kangourou
kangaroo

une tortue
turtle

un crocodile
crocodile

un dauphin
dolphin

une baleine
whale

un poisson
fish

une étoile de mer
starfish

un crabe
crab

un coquillage
seashell

un tracteur
tractor

une moissonneuse-batteuse
combine

une pelleteuse
digger

un bulldozer
bulldozer

une grue
crane

un camion
lorry

une voiture
car

une roue
wheel

une moto
motorbike

un casque
crash helmet

une bicyclette
bicycle

une sonnette
bell

un hélicopter
helicopter

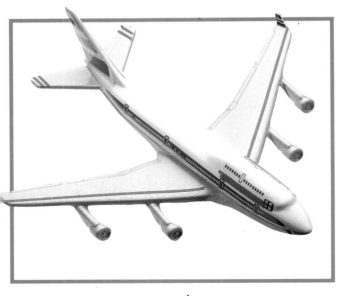

un avion
plane

un bateau à voile
sailing boat

une vedette
speed boat

une carte postale
postcard

un colis
parcel

une carte d'anniversaire
birthday card

une enveloppe
envelope

du papier-cadeau
wrapping paper

un ruban
ribbon

un noeud
bow

un cadeau
present

Index

Doll's house furniture by courtesy of
Rainbow, 253 Archway Road, London N6 5BS
and the Singing Tree, 69 New King's Road, London SW6 4SQ

First published in Great Britain in 1994 by
Frances Lincoln Limited, Apollo Works
5 Charlton Kings Road, London NW5 2SB

Published by arrangement with Père Castor-Flammarion, Paris

British Library Cataloguing in Publication Data
available on request

ISBN 0-7112-0876-X

Set in Helvetica by FMT
Printed and bound in Hong Kong

1 3 5 7 9 8 6 4 2